The Gypsies

The Gypsies

WERNER COHN
University of British Columbia

ADDISON-WESLEY PUBLISHING COMPANY
Reading, Massachusetts
Menlo Park, California · London · Don Mills, Ontario

This book is in the
Addison-Wesley Modular Program in Anthropology

ISBN 0-201-11362-7
ABCDEFGHIJ-CO-79876543

About the Author

Werner Cohn received the B.S.S. degree from City College of New York and the M.A. and Ph.D. degrees from the New School for Social Research. He is at present Professor of Sociology at the University of British Columbia. He specializes in the sociology of Gypsies and Jews.

Contents

Introduction

My earliest memory of a Gypsy is also one of the
earliest memories of my childhood. I am very
hazy now about the details; I remember my impression much more than I remember what actually occurred. I was about six years old, a
Jewish boy in Berlin where Hitler had just come
to power. On that day, which I now realize was
the beginning of my interest in Gypsies, I was in
a small branch post office, probably loitering
rather than doing anything recognizably purposeful.
The Gypsy woman was dressed as Gypsies are
often pictured in books, and I must have stared at
her curiously. I suppose that I must also have had
some feelings of superiority. Having lived in an
environment in which peoples were judged as in-
ferior or superior, I am sure that my stare must
have contained a certain satisfaction at seeing
someone considered to be even lower than the Jews.
I do not recall the exact words of that Gypsy woman,
but I know she said something to the effect that
"dirty little Jewish boys should mind their own

Photo taken at a camp of *Rom* outside Belgrade, Yugoslavia, 1969

business. " I also know that in addition to my feeling of injury, I was startled by the effectiveness of
her thrust, by her self-confidence, by her disregard of the social conventions according to which
Gypsies were considered to be the lowest form of
human life.

Not everyone in our society has had personal
experiences with Gypsies, but virtually everyone
is subjected to a certain stereotype that is perpe-
tuated in thousands of articles, popular books, and
motion pictures.

There are two distinct images in this stereotype. On the one hand, Gypsies are thought to
steal, to lead a shiftless life, to be unreliable,
dangerous, dirty. Almost all people who have
grown up in southern and eastern Europe were told
in their childhood to stay away from Gypsies because Gyspies abduct children. However, there is
not a single authenticated case of abduction by
Gypsies, though there are cases, such as that of
Jan Yoors (Yoors, 1967), in which youngsters have
run away from home in order to travel with Gypsies[1] [all notes appear at the conclusion of the text].

The other popular image of Gypsies is more
benign but no more realistic. It is said that Gypsies are gay, musical, free-spirited, romantic.
John Masefield relied on this notion in his poem
Sea-Fever: "I must go down to the seas again to
the vagrant gypsy life... "

In any case, the stereotype of Gypsy life is
fairly firmly established in our language. The
verb "to gyp, " in the sense of "to swindle, cheat,
or steal" is frequently used by people who would
not dream of saying "he jewed me down, " and the
thesaurus lists synonyms of the word "gypsy" as
wanderer, roamer, vagabond, knight of the road.

Photo taken at a camp of *Rom* outside Bucarest, Romania, summer 1969

The professional sociological literature is not exempt from unscholarly reliance on this stereotype in the treatment of Gypsies. One of the most prestigious of social scientists, contributing to an anthology of very high professional standards, uses Gypsies as an illustration for his discussion of criminals. The author of a widely quoted recent book on Gypsies, by his own admission, cannot understand the Gypsy language. The text is a mixture of fact and romantic fiction, culled from similarly produced earlier works, and some superficial contacts with French Gypsies. In my professional career, I have never encountered a subject treated as poorly in standard works of reference.

Unfortunately, scholarly work in the field of Gypsy studies is very difficult. One can hardly encourage an interested graduate student to plan fieldwork among people with whom he is unlikely to establish adequate rapport within a reasonable period of time. Learning the Gypsy language is no more difficult than learning most other languages, and much easier than many; however, the problem lies in finding someone able and willing to teach it. Similar difficulties face the professional anthropologist who is eager to get at least some results after a year or two of effort. It is to the lasting credit of Rena Cotten Gropper (Cotten, 1950) that she overcame these difficulties as a young graduate student, and thus established herself as the first scholarly observer of Gypsies in North America.

The following discussion will outline the procedures of my own work and the nature of the data I have gathered.

Methods of Study

Until the academic year of 1966-1967, my research interests centered on the sociology of Jews and of certain small religious groups. (As a graduate student, I had done a thesis on Jehovah's Witnesses.) In general, I was interested in groups that live within our society but which, in one way or another, have become excluded from full participation in it. I believe that a study of these groups helps us to understand our society and culture. In 1966, my family and I went to France for a sabbatical year; my major purpose there was to study small Protestant sects in the Paris region. But while in Paris, I came in contact with the organization Etudes Tsiganes. This is a semiofficial group of social workers, scholars, and others interested in Gypsies. They publish a journal under the same name, organize lectures and discussions, and, in general, make it possible for the public to come into contact with authentic Gypsy studies. It is through this group that I received my first orientation and background in the technical literature concerning Gypsies.

When I returned to Canada in the fall of 1967, I was determined to begin fieldwork with Gypsies there. My readings and brief contacts in France had convinced me of the importance of learning the Gypsy language (a judgment that all my subsequent experience has confirmed). I thus needed to find Gypsies willing to talk with me and to teach me the language.

My first steps were straightforward. I went to Vancouver's oldest business section, which was then a rather run-down neighborhood of secondhand stores, cheap restaurants, derelicts, and drug addicts. I had been told that a number of Gypsy fortune-telling establishments could be found there. After an hour or two of searching, I finally located what I later learned was an ofisa, a storefront fortune-telling location. The door was locked, and the view of the store was blocked to the outside by a variety of curtains. (Cotten, 1950, contains descriptions and floor plans of similar establishments in New York City.)

I knocked on the door and was met by a young woman who, with something of a smirk, proposed to tell me my fortune. Since I could sense even then the folly of any attempt by a male fieldworker to confer with young Gypsy women, I explained to her that I wanted to meet her husband or father. She told me abruptly that no one was home and shut the door in my face.

I returned several times that day, and the woman got more hostile each time. Once she demanded that I tell her what I wanted to see her husband for. When I told her that I was interested in learning the Gypsy language, her tone of voice switched briefly from one of hostility to one of

Photo taken outside an *ofisa* in Vancouver, British Columbia

giving information; she told me I would not be able
to learn the language. I was told also to leave, and
not to come back.

I had heard that Gypsies are often involved with
the law, and thought that the police might know
where to find some others. The detectives of the
fraud squad were cooperative and pleasant. They
told me many things concerning the method of
operation of fortune tellers. (Some of these police
reports are very informative; the very good article
by Mitchell, 1955, is based on such sources.)
The detectives furnished me with the names and
addresses of several Gypsies, one of whom I pro-
ceeded to visit. I was again and repeatedly put off
by the man's wife, and had just about decided, as
must have many other would-be fieldworkers with
Gypsies, that no rapport was possible. The woman's
function as keeper of the gate was well esteblished.

However, before giving up completely, I decided to make a final gesture. I wrote a letter on
University stationery to the man whose name had
been given to me by the police, explaining that I
would like to learn the Gypsy language and was
willing to pay for lessons. Several days later I
received a telephone call from this man, telling me
that his father would be willing to give me these
lessons.

Thus started a long relationship with my first
principal informant, whom I shall call Stevano,
which was unbroken until his death three years
later. The regular language lessons with Stevano
lasted an average of an hour and a half each, one
to three times weekly. Since Stevano's death, I
have had similar sessions with his oldest son, whom
I shall call Vania. Altogether, I have so far done
four and a half years of this kind of fieldwork.

When I first started my work with Stevano, I did not know a single word of the Gypsy language. Moreover, I had had no experience in learning an unwritten language, no linguistic training, and no courses in linguistic fieldwork. A linguist colleague kindly helped me overcome some of these deficiencies by providing concentrated tutoring. I was also aided by the little vade mecum which had just appeared, by Sarah C. Gudschinsky (1967).

I taped all my sessions with Stevano, and went over them at home until I slowly began to grasp the skeleton of the language. The wonderful description of the language by Gjerdman and Ljungberg (1963), a work of extraordinary thoroughness and scholarship, is always at my side; I keep one copy at home for study and reference, another one at my office in order to look up matters that come to my mind during the day.

My conversations with Stevano and Vania dealt not only with the Gypsy language but also with whatever other aspect of Gypsy life and culture might occur to one of us. But in addition to such free-ranging discussion, I was involved in a number of more formal projects in these sessions. One was the recording of several folk tales told by Stevano in the Gypsy language and then annotated by the two of us. (See Cohn, 1972a, for one of these tales.) In another project I obtained Vania's responses to the Thematic Apperception Test (a psychological instrument for assessing personality), again in the Gypsy language. This project actually took several months, since I followed the same procedures I had used in taking down Stevano's stories. After the initial recording of Vania's responses (twenty stories created by him to explain the TAT pictures), I played back the tape, and together with him recorded in writing each word he had spoken. This project not only gave me a great deal of insight into Vania's personality, but also gave a substantial boost to my competence in the language.

In another systematic line of questioning Stevano (and some others), I obtained the kinship terms as used in the American dialect of the Gypsy language and related these findings to what I knew of Gypsy culture (Cohn, 1969). This proved to be extremely rewarding in furthering my understanding; I will draw on these results in the section on "Kinship Terminology and the Bride-Price."

My latest project, and most elaborate so far, consisted of asking Vania and others about genealogies. The work became so complicated that I had to use a computer to help me sort out the results. I had learned from Vania and a number of other Gypsies in various parts of North America something about the meaning of <u>vitsi</u> (tribes) among Gypsies. An individual Gypsy holds his own and allied tribes to be more desirable for purposes of social contact and intermarriage than other tribes. This is a matter of attitudes, and I had established these preferences to my own satisfaction (Cohn, n.d.). But while I knew how Gypsies would prefer marriages to take place, I also knew that the actual practice might very well differ. For that reason I decided to research the details of actual marriages. If I could obtain the tribal affiliations of the partners for as many marriages as possible, I would then be able to determine how actual marriage alignments correspond to the expressed preferences of my various informants. (As I soon discovered, family networks, much more than tribal affiliations, determine marriages. See below, "Inbreeding and the Bride-Price.")

But to satisfy certain other curiosities on my part, I wanted to discover more than merely records of marriages. I had started my fieldwork knowing that I would have to learn the Gypsy language. As my work progressed, I began to see one other area of knowledge that I would have to try to assimilate in order to understand anything at all about Gypsies: the various patterns of family relationships among the Gypsy people I met. Much of the conversation and concern among Gypsies deals with marriages, relationships among relatives, and friendships and enmities that arise from these alliances. Without knowing how individuals are related to one another, the fieldworker simply cannot understand the concerns and anxieties that preoccupy the minds of the Gypsies. Moreover, in order to gain acceptance by Gypsies in other cities, I had found that I must demonstrate a more or less intimate knowledge of family networks as well as a knowledge of the language.

To satisfy these various needs, I devised a procedure that now allows me to feed into the computer information on individuals, and their marriages and their respective parents, and to obtain information on how everyone is related to everyone else. The program can also tell me how many individuals of each tribe married individuals from every other tribe, and the extent to which grooms and brides may be related as cousins or other relatives. (The actual program was written by my research assistant, Mr. Lewis James, for use with the IBM 360-67 at the University of British Columbia.) The data base in my computer file grows each time I receive more information from Vania or from another Gypsy. At the moment of this writing, I have information on 484 individuals with birth dates

A Gypsy man and his grandsons, in a west coast U. S. city

ranging from 1830 to 1970, and on 199 marriages
contracted between 1848 and 1970.

Although my sessions with Stevano and Vania
constitute the most important source of my understanding of Gypsies, it has been necessary to sup-
plement this source in various ways. My wife and
I make it a practice to attend Gypsy feasts (weddings,
funerals, saint's days) as often as we can. There
it is possible to meet a great many other Gypsies,
to observe social interaction among them, and to
take pictures.

I have made trips to a number of other cities
in North America, meeting Gypsies, observing
business patterns, attending feasts, taking pictures,
discussing family networks, gathering genealogical
data. These cities include New York (in the summer, several scores of Gypsies may be found in
the Coney Island amusement area), Montreal,
Seattle, Portland, San Francisco, and New Orleans.

In the summer of 1969, and again in 1970, I
traveled to Europe to observe Gypsy groups there,
to meet most of the experts who are engaged in
Gypsy studies, and to take pictures and tape-record
samples of the various Gypsy dialects. I have done
this work in France, Austria, Sweden, Yugoslavia,
Romania, Czechoslovakia, Hungary, Poland, the
Soviet Union, Bulgaria, and Turkey. These trips
were made possible through grants from the Canada
Council. On a different occasion, I also visited
Gypsy camps in England and in Germany.

The pictures I have taken in various parts of
the world (this collection amounts to about 1200
slides, a number of which are reproduced here)
have been of great help to me in understanding certain aspects of Gypsy life. For instance, I have
hundreds of slides which I took at weddings and

English Gypsy children near London, January 1970

other functions. It was possible for me to study,
through them, something of the pattern of men-
women interactions at these events, as well as the
role of children in Gypsy life.

Finally, I must say something about my personal relationship with my informants. More by
necessity than by choice, I have always remained
an outsider, although I am given credit for knowing
more than other outsiders and for not being dangerous, as a detective would be considered. But
my informants have never become friends in the
sense in which this term ordinarily applies. I
pay five dollars for each session with Vania and
did the same with his father. We see one another
more frequently than I see any of my friends, but
no very strong personal relationship has developed.
Despite many invitations, Gypsies have visited my
home only once--briefly before Stevano's death, he
and two of his sons came to look at my slides of
Gypsies in Europe. My wife and I get invitations
to many Gypsy functions, but so do certain other
non-Gypsies with whom the Gypsies do business:
car salesmen, social workers, detectives. The
sacred separation between Gypsy and gaZo (outsider), which in my view is one of the central fea-
tures of Gypsy life, is essentially maintained. This
aspect of fieldwork with Gypsies often makes the
research emotionally taxing, and may well be an
important reason which has deterred professional
social scientists from serious work with Gypsies.

The Varieties of Gypsies

Despite the existence of certain in-between groups
like the Tinkers of Britain and the Jenisch of Germany, fairly clear-cut and generally accepted cri-
teria suggest themselves for the determination of
who is and who is not a Gypsy. The situation is
particularly clear in North America, which has a
well-defined, self-conscious Gypsy cultural group.
These people call themselves Rom, speak a highly
inflected Indic language which they call Romanes,
and have assimilated most other individuals who
have come here from Europe and who continue to
lead any sort of Gypsy life. It is of course these
Rom with whose culture and style of life I am acquainted at first hand.

In Europe, the situation is somewhat more
complex. First of all, I found Rom in almost all
the countries I visited. I was able to converse in
the dialect I had learned in Vancouver in suburbs
of Paris, in the center of Moscow, on the roads of
Romania; the style of life of these people was also
similar to that of the Gypsies in North America.

Photo taken at a camp of *Rom* outside Bucarest, Romania, summer 1969

On the other hand, each European country also has
sizable numbers of different types of Gypsies,
which, with the possible exception of Romania,
probably outnumber the Rom.

France has three major types of Gypsies: the
Rom, the Spanish Gypsies, and the manuS. Spanish
Gypsies speak a dialect of Spanish with some admixture of vocabulary from Indic sources; these
people seem to form the majority of the Gypsies of
Spain, but have never been, to my knowledge,
satisfactorily studied.

The manuS are known as sinti in Germany. We
now have fairly good descriptions of their language
(Jean, 1970; Calvet, Delvoye, and Labalette, 1970),
which is similar to Romanes but has many Germanic
vocabulary items. I have visited with these people
in both Germany and France, and have observed
many similarities with the Rom, such as fortune-
telling, the sale of trinkets to non-Gypsies, a semi-
nomadic life. There are, however, also some important differences. Many of these people are
musicians, which is not the case with Rom. The
manuS are also much more frequently involved with
Christian missionary efforts, especially with those
of the Pentecostal churches. On the whole, the
manuS give a much more acculturated impression;
they seem much friendlier to outsiders than do the
Rom, and are certainly easier to talk with upon
casual contact.

The Balkans and Eastern Europe have a great
variety of Gypsies in various stages of assimilation
to their surrounding cultures. In Yugoslavia, for
instance, I have seen traveling Rom and highly
assimilated Gypsy factory workers; there is also
a very small group of educated Gypsies in that
country. (I have met an army officer, a school-

teacher, a young poet, an engineer, and several
well-known entertainers.) The linguistic situation
is particularly diversified. Some of the groups I
have visited speak Romanes, others a language
related to Turkish, still others speak Romanian.
(These languages, there as well as everywhere
else, are spoken in addition to the national languages of the countries in which the Gypsies live.)
      Romanian-speaking Gypsies form a special
group found in countries other than the Balkans.
The Rom call these people boiaS and sometimes
the two groups intermarry. I have met a family
of boiaS in Paris, where they work as exhibitors
of trained animals in carnivals; in Yugoslavia, they
put on sidewalk performances with trained bears.
Most of the American boiaS seem to have assimilated with the Rom, but I visited a roadside camp
in Louisiana where I met about thirty boiaS families. The term they use to describe their own
group is ludar. The physical appearance of these
people was very similar to that of the Rom, but
they conversed only in English among themselves.
Some of the older people still knew Romanian.
Among the artifacts they showed me were a thirteen-
year old directory of the Romanian Orthodox Church
in America, a Romanian-English dictionary, and
a bible in Romanian. They explained to me that
their work consists of operating independent con-
cessions at carnivals, and they thus travel all the
time. The camp I visited was their winter resi-
dence. (These Romanian-speaking people are not
to be confused with other groups, for instance the
Rom, whose Gypsy language shows strong Romanian vocabulary influences.)
      Hungary, Romania, Czechoslovakia, Yugosla-
via, and Bulgaria all have substantial Gypsy

A *boiaš* bear leader, in Niš, Yugoslavia, summer 1969

minorities, but these Gypsies are culturally very heterogeneous. The Hungarian Gypsy musicians, for instance, seem to form a caste-like group of their own, handing their musical occupations down through the generations. The people of this group whom I met no longer spoke any form of the Gypsy language (we conversed in German), but they assured me that their grandparents still spoke Gypsy. They also gave me examples of Gypsy expressions which they still use in their work--terms referring to the tempo and loudness of the music.

The Gypsies of Britain and those of Spain form special cultural islands. Their respective dialects, because of the loss of Indic inflections, must be considered dialects of English and Spanish. As far as I know, no substantial recent anthropological or linguistic work has been done with either group (the language described by Sampson, 1926, is no longer spoken). Students of Gypsy culture all over the world will be much indebted to anyone willing to undertake this task.

The word "Gypsy," finally, is sometimes used to describe certain traveling people in India and other parts of Asia. Since the European environment and European languages have had such profound influence on the people I have mentioned so far, I prefer to use the word "Gypsy" only for those groups who, while showing evidence of Indic origins in language and appearance, have a history of inter-relationships with European peoples.

Although the literature is full of various guesses, the total number of Gypsies in the world is difficult to estimate. A report by an agency of the British government (Ministry of Housing and Local Government, 1967, p. 58) surveys various censuses and estimates, and gives figures that total to about

1,200,000. But this survey does not include all
countries in which Gypsies may be found in sizable
numbers; Spain, in particular, is not included, and
neither is Turkey.

The figures given for the United States are
"50-100,000. " When I looked up the article cited
as authority for this estimate, it turned out to
have been written by my friend Rena Cotten Gropper,
who I found had cited these figures as examples of
mistaken judgments, and had given her own estimate
as somewhere between 100,000 and 300,000. In
my opinion, the numbers must be much smaller,
probably around 20,000, since almost all the Gypsy
adults I have met anywhere in North America know
of nearly all the other families I have met.

The largest concentration of North American
Gypsies is probably in the New York City area.
Police sources there have estimated about 1000
fortune-telling establishments, which would seem
to indicate a population of about 4000 Gypsies.
However, since Gypsies travel a good deal, this
figure would fluctuate from time to time.

The British survey lists Bulgaria as reporting
about three percent of its 1965 population as Gypsy.
The Romanian census figures for 1956, showing
only 0.6 percent as Gypsy, are almost certainly an
underestimate, as are the other official statistics
from Balkan countries. Because of their style of
life, Gypsies are more diffiuult to enumerate than
others; moreover, there is almost certainly a
tendency for many Gypsies to report themselves
to the census takers as belonging to some tther
ethnic group.

The conventional literature on Gypsies often
makes a distinction between "nomadic" and "sedentary" Gypsies. In my opinion, this distinction is

not very meaningful, at least not for the Gypsies
whom I have observed. The travelers with whom
I spent some time in Romania have homes where
they live in the winter, so that they are both nomadic and sedentary, depending on the season.
A family of settled Gypsies in Belgrade, whom I
visit whenever I am in that city, has members who
travel to tourist spots in the summer to sell trinkets. American Rom constantly move around (for
feasts, or to establish fortune-telling parlors for
a season or two) but are known, at the same time,
as regular longtime residents of a particular city.
My principal informants have been residents of
Vancouver for about thirty years, but this has not
prevented them from being "nomadic" at the same
time. Of course those Gypsy groups in the Balkans
that have become more or less assimilated to non-
Gypsy life (the factory workers, in particular)
cannot be called travelers. But insofar as Gypsies
lead a Gypsy style of life, it is most misleading
to speak of a "sedentary" status.

Finally, and in summary of this brief survey
of different Gypsy groups, I would like to observe
the following:

1.   The various Gypsy groups in Europe and
America may be classified as either more or less
localized in a particular area of Europe, or as
being dispersed throughout the European and American culture area.

2.   The Rom are probably the most widely dispersed
group. The Gypsies of Spain and Britain, and many
smaller groups found in the Balkans and in eastern
Europe, are rather strictly localized. The boiaS
and the manuS (sinti) hold intermediary positions.

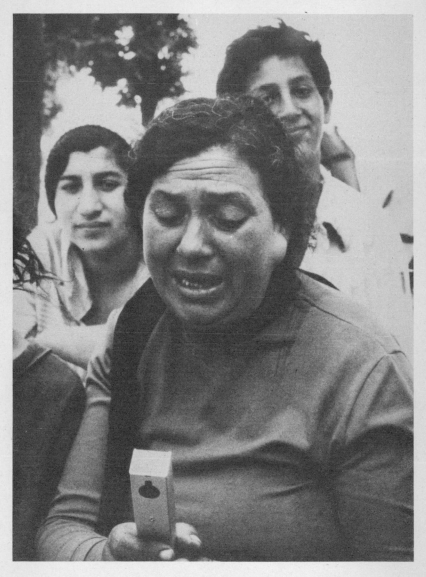

Romni (woman *Rom*) singing a traditional Gypsy song into the author's tape recorder, Timișoara, Romania, summer 1970

3.   The cultural integrity of the <u>Rom</u> seems more intact than that of the other groups. Gypsy life in North America, where the <u>Rom</u> are on the whole the only Gypsy group, has a vigor and integrity unsurpassed anywhere else in the world. In particular, there do not seem to be the kind of assimilatory pressures here that operate on the much larger Gypsy groups in the Balkans.

Gypsy Origins

The history of the Gypsies is not very clear. Gypsies are not very literate people; to this day, even
in the United States, a great many cannot read or
write. They have no records of their own. Their
language is unwritten (except, of course, when it is
reduced to writing by non-Gypsy scholars). Whatever we know of their background comes from two
sources: the linguistic evidence, which unambi-
guously points to India, and scattered references
in European documents (decrees, church records,
court records) which have been collected and ana-
lyzed by Vaux de Foletier (1970).

All dialects spoken by Gypsy groups show Indic
influences. The language of the Rom and manuS,
as well as that of certain other groups, is particularly close to the Indo-European languages of India
in vocabulary, and even more so in grammar and
phonology. This evidence leaves no doubt that the
first Gypsies came to Europe from India. Beyond
that, the language shows lexical traces of Middle
Eastern languages, especially of Persian, Kurdish,

and Armenian, and considerable influences of
Greek vocabulary. We can conclude that all the
Gypsy groups whose languages have been studied
have probably spent some time in Middle Eastern
and Greek language areas.

Beyond this basic material in all the Gypsy
languages and dialects, the groups show variation.
The Rom speak a language which some European
scholars classify within the vlax group of Gypsy
dialects, named after the Romanian province of
Wallachia, because of a very strong admixture of
Romanian lexical items. Other Gypsy dialects
lack this particular influence. We must conclude
from this and other evidence that the Rom, but not
all the other groups, are descendants of people
who lived in Romanian language areas for considerable periods of time.

Vaux de Foletier found the first references to
Gypsies in European documents of the fourteenth
century; hence we can say that Gypsies have lived
among European peoples for at least 600 years.
The old documents are worth looking at for the
remarkable cultural similarity which they disclose
between the earliest known Gypsies in Europe and
Their descendants of today. In general, these
people were travelers, the women told fortunes to
the indigenous population, and there were minor
tensions between Gypsies and non-Gypsies throughout the centuries. Such tensions had to do with the
Gypsies' begging, petty crime, theft of chickens,
and so forth. There were also numerous rumors
of kidnapping, to which I have already referred.
(For a discussion of this theme in European literature, see Vaux de Foletier, 1970, pp. 66ff.)

The literature speaks of the enslavement of
Gypsies in Romania between the fourteenth and

nineteenth centuries (Vaux de Foletier, 1970, pp.
86ff.). I cannot evaluate the nature of the social
conditions under which Gypsies lived there during
this long period, but it seems clear that the legal
emancipation that took place in the Romanian ter-
ritories in the middle of the nineteenth century,
allowing the former slaves to leave, precipitated
a wave of migration of these Romanian Gypsies
toward Russia, Austria, Serbia, Western Europe,
and ultimately America. As I have already remarked, the Rom and similar groups that I found
in Russia, France, Sweden, and of course North
America, all have a great many Romanian vocabulary items in their language.

While there were small numbers of Gypsies
of various types on the North American continent
before this migration, the Rom of today can be
substantially traced to immigrants who came to
this hemisphere around the end of the nineteenth
century. The grandfathers of my middle-aged
informants were born in Serbia, Austria, or
Russia; I have no report of Romania as a birth-
place. It would seem that at least two generations
separated the Romanian emigrants from the American immigrants. The wandering life of these
immediate forebears of the American Rom must have
have been very similar to that described, for those
Gypsies of a much later period, by Yoors (1967).
In many cases, a grandmother is reported as having
been born in Russia, a grandfather in Serbia, or
vice versa, for those who migrated over relatively
large areas would often meet and intermarry.

Two of the three major dialects in the language
of the American Rom of today derive from particular areas of Europe. One of these is the "Russian"
dialect; another is the dialect of Macva, a Serbian-

speaking area of Austria-Hungary before the First World War; the third dialect is simply called "Coppersmith," referring to a very large subgroup of Rom in Europe and America. But all these dialects belong to the particular vlax (Romanian-influenced) language of the Rom; a few rather rare vocabulary items aside, the dialects are mutually intelligible.

In brief, the respective Serbian and Russian accretions, on a more common Romanian base, on top of a still more common basic Indic language with some Middle Eastern and Greek elements, give a fairly good indication of the origins of the North American Rom.

Life of the *Rom*

Vania, the son of my first Gypsy informant Stevano, is now forty-eight years old. His wife, whom I shall call Duda, is eight years younger. Duda is actually Vania's fourth wife, but this serial monogamy of Vania's is no more typical of the Gypsies than it is of North American non-Gypsies. It is in fact probably much rarer, the bride-price serving to stabilize marriages. Vania is Duda's first husband.

Vania and Duda live with their two young daughters, aged four and thirteen, in a very small apartment in the central business section. The apartment is also used for fortune-telling during the day, with Duda often sitting in the downstairs entrance to the building in order to solicit clients. The thirteen-year-old daughter has not yet started to tell fortunes, despite some urging from her parents to do so.

Vania spends much of his time on the telephone, arranging the sale of used cars or just talking with friends and relatives. Much of the talk and gossip

Gypsy feast in Vancouver, British Columbia, 1970

with other Gypsies concerns affairs of bride-price:
how much so-and-so paid, how much is owing, how
much can be expected soon.

Another very important topic of conversation
concerns the frequent Gypsy feasts. Feasts are
given for saint's days using an adaptation of the
Serbian Orthodox calendar which has been handed
down verbally through the generations. They are
also given for weddings and to honor someone who
has recently died, or simply one who is visiting
town. In all cases rather elaborate arrangements
are made to rent a hall, to do the cooking, to
arrange for food and liquor supplies. A feast is
generally sponsored jointly by two or three brothers
who undertake to pay all the expenses. At a marriage, guests contribute to a collection, which
helps to reimburse the father of the groom for
both the bride-price and the expenses of the feast.

All feasts feature sumptuous but hasty eating,
slow drinking, and, except for the memorial feasts,
dancing. The men do most of the cooking, the
women the serving and cleaning up. Although men
and women eat and dance separately, individuals
often feel free to chat briefly with their spouses
or with other persons of the opposite sex. Sometimes young people have some mixed dancing, but
the general rule is for the sexes to remain separated. Rather more frequently than not, the feasts
also furnish opportunities to renew animosities
with other Gypsies; these grudges most often concern unresolved problems of bride-price. The
participation of all age groups is a most striking
feature of the feasts. The very youngest roam
around the hall with a great deal of freedom,
helping themselves to food, playing with the elec-
tronic musical equipment, chasing one another.

Roasting lambs for a feast in Vancouver, British Columbia, 1970

People very frequently travel hundreds of miles to attend these feasts, for they form a highlight of Gypsy life.

But I have also seen a great deal of boredom and drabness in the Gypsy lifestyle. Vania's little girls sit in front of the television set all day. Parents do not very strenuously encourage the children to attend school, and in localities in which the number of Gypsies is small, the children do not have much else to do but watch television and accompany their parents on shopping expeditions. Vania's girls do have cousins in the city with whom they play from time to time, but I do not believe that they ever play with non-Gypsy children.

The daily life of elderly Gypsies is sometimes full of sadness and frustration. Before he died, Stevano used to complain bitterly to me that his children had abandoned him, that they did not show enough interest in his welfare. I do know, however, that he either saw his sons or spoke with them on the phone daily. I have met other old people in New Orleans and New York who seemed to me similarly forlorn and unhappy, complaining of insufficient contact with their children. Yet such contacts are actually quite frequent, if not in person, at least by telephone. The amount of long-distance telephoning is astounding; families I visit always seem to be engaged in transcontinental phone calls. Duda talks to her parents, 3000 miles away, several times a week. Yet her father complained to me quite bitterly that he does not hear enough from her.

All the Gypsy women whom I know tell fortunes. The word for fortune-telling is drabarimos; it is most probably related to another Gypsy word, drab, which means medicine. But in the minds of the Gypsies, the activity is not thought of as rendering

a service to the public; it is a means of earning,
or more accurately of extracting, money from
non-Gypsies. The idea that there could be any
validity in what the fortune-teller tells the client
is generally ridiculous to the Gypsies. When I
press my informants on this point, they will allow
that there have been Gypsy women who have been
able to help people, but such wise old women no
longer seem to be around. It would be considered
most shameful for a Gypsy of either sex to have
his fortune told by a Gypsy woman, even if one of
ability could be found. In this respect I am considered as a Gypsy; it is unlikely, in fact, that any
attempt at fortune-telling would be made to any
outsider who is at all acquainted with a Gypsy
family.

Fortunes are told in special storefront ofisuria,
in booths or tents at fairs and amusement parks,
and in the homes and apartments where the Gypsies
live. Wherever fortune-telling is done, certain
props are in evidence: statues of saints, bibles,
pictures of Jesus and the saints. But the Gypsies
are attached to such artifacts over and above their
usefulness in the fortune-telling business; there
is, as a result, a certain ambivalence in regard
to such religious items. One of my informants
once remarked that such objects are there only to
impress the outsiders; another, an older man, was
offended by this cynicism and insisted on regarding
these articles as beneficial to himself and his family.

The religious items are placed primarily where
the outsiders would see them. But I have also seen
them in bedrooms where no outsider would be per-
mitted. In his bedroom, Stevano had a large picture of the Last Supper, which he would drape at

Gypsy children at an impromptu party in California, 1968

certain times. He was reluctant to explain why the picture was draped, but from what his son told me later, I understand that Stevano would have considered it unseemly to appear without clothes before a picture of Jesus.

Generally, Gypsy men do not tell fortunes. I have seen one do so in a very peremptory manner at Coney Island; he was filling in for his wife in looking after the booth. But this is quite exceptional. Telling fortunes is strictly woman's business, done in a woman's way; the skill is handed down from mother to daughter.

There are several styles of fortune-telling. Gypsies have a keen appreciation of the varieties of attributes of gaZe ("outsiders") which make them suitable as fortune-telling clients: lasciviousness, greed, superstition, loneliness. On the other hand, there are also different types of fortune-tellers: the woman may be young or old or middle-aged; she may work in the central business area or in the suburbs; as a permanent resident of the city, she may have good working relations with the police, or, on the contrary, she may be in town only temporarily. The style of fortune-telling adapts itself to all these variations.

Young women fortune-tellers invariably take advantage of the lasciviousness of male clients. Gypsy women who sit in the windows of the storefront ofisuria, or, as in midtown Manhattan, in open doorways leading to lofts which are used as residences and fortune-telling establishments, beckon to passers-by in the manner of prostitutes. In some localities the establishments are disguised as shoe-shine parlors, with young Gypsy women offering to shine shoes as a prelude to telling fortunes. The implied sexual promises are never

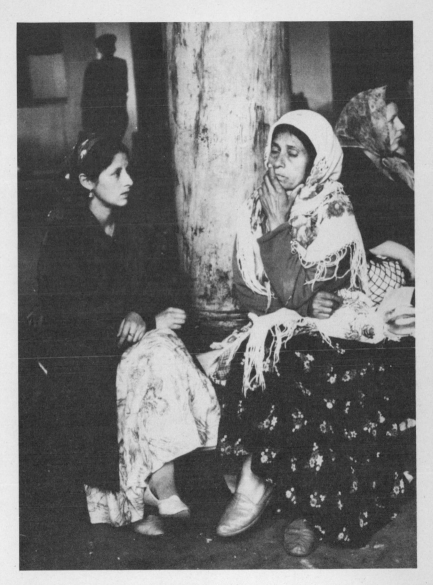

Gypsy fortune tellers in the Moravian Railroad Station, Moscow, 1970

carried through, but cases are known in which
wallets have been lifted in the course of some pro-
vocative scuffling. When clients complain, the
situation is handled either by the counterthreat of
a rape complaint, by restitution of the money, or
by a combination of these two methods. But these
rough methods are reserved for rough localities
(for instance, the Times Square area) and to tran-
sient fortune-tellers. Much more usual are methods
by which, in return for three or five dollars, the
gaZo ("outsider") is given some soothing talk and
is sent on his way.

Older women fortune-tellers emphasize the
role of the wise advisor. Problems of health,
love, and finances are comfortingly discussed with
the client, who is often an older woman herself.
Cases are known in which the fortune-teller skill-
fully establishes a relationship of dependence on
the part of the client, and is able to extract considerable sums of money. I have in my possession
the 4600 pages of transcript of a trial which took
place in New York City from January to April of
1962 (People vs. Volga Adams), in which it was
alleged, but not proven, that a Gypsy fortune-teller
known as Volga Adams had obtained the sum of
$118,000 from a woman in her late forties who had
been under stress of loneliness and emotional tension, and who had begun to rely on the fortune-
teller as a sympathetic listener and advisor. But
it should be emphasized here too that Gypsy confidence cases involving thousands of dollars are
extremely rare. Most fortune-tellers make a few
dollars on a client, and sometimes have more or
less steady customers who bring in a steady trickle
of funds, but do not try for any large sum of money.
This attitude is also influenced by the fact that

Fortune tellers at Concy Island, New York, 1970

fortune-tellers are almost invariably known to the
local police, who simply do not tolerate large and
spectacular swindles. (One method that is occasionally used to obtain a large amount of money is
called buZo, "small bag, " after the implement in
which the client is asked to deposit his savings so
that these can be "blessed." For descriptions of
such methods, see Mitchell, 1955.)

Another activity of Gypsy girls and women,
very close in spirit and method to fortune-telling,
is begging through the sale of artificial flowers in
the streets. In areas like Times Square of New
York, and North Beach and Fisherman's Wharf in
San Francisco, Gypsy women (and sometimes boys)
accost well-dressed young couples who are obviously
out on important dates. The method consists of
pinning a cheap artificial flower (worth a few cents)
on the lady; when the man asks for the price, the
Gypsy will calmly name a figure in the neighborhood of two dollars, relying on the gallant's em-
barrassment for a swift completion of the sale.
I have been told that quite a bit of money can be
acquired in that way.

Of all Gypsy activities, fortune-telling is at
the same time the most traditional and the most
widespread; old Gypsy women and young, rich and
poor, prominent and unknown, all tell fortunes.
It is way of making money, but also the way of
being a Gypsy woman. In the Gypsy language there
is a word for work, buki, but it is never applied
to the activity of telling fortunes--buki is the business of the men.

I have heard it said of many older Gypsy men
that they have never worked in their lives. This
seems to be true of most, perhaps all, Gypsy
males, if "work" is thought of as involving a

continuing and regular responsibility. However,
most of the men do arrange many aspects of the
fortune-telling business. They will place ads in
the classified section of newspapers ("Madam
Laura, gifted reader, she will help you with all
your problems"), arrange for the printing and distribution of handbills to advertise the fortune-
telling, and deal with landlords to arrange for
locations.

But the major work of the men consists of a
complex of activities that I would call "Gypsy
business." It takes several forms but in its fun-
damental spirit and method it is actually only one.
This Gypsy business is as much the way of being
a Gypsy man as fortune-telling is the way of being
a Gypsy woman. The most important form of
Gypsy business, involving almost all the men, is
now the purchase and resale of used cars and
trailers. Other forms are fender work, obtaining
relief payments, and police work.

The used-car business is almost invariably
carried on by placing ads in the classified section
of newspapers; the Gypsies almost never bother
to obtain business licenses. Purchases seem to be
done mainly through connections with established
non-Gypsy wholesalers. I have had frequent occasion to be present at sales to customers. The at-
mosphere of these transactions is not very different from that of ordinary used-car lots. Older
Gypsies proudly tell stories of how their fathers
and grandfathers used to sell horses, using a
variety of tricks to make a bad horse look like a
good one. The car sales now are carried on in this
same tradition.

Most of the Gypsies I know are on relief rolls.
Since the irregular cash flow from fortune-telling

and selling cars does not leave the traces of a
regular income, relief agencies generally find
themselves forced to accept the Gypsies' claims
of indigence.

In speaking of police work, we reach an area
of moral ambiguity. Most Gypsies, perhaps all,
have some dealings with the police as a result of
the fortune-telling activities of the women. I have
very little evidence concerning direct payoffs, but
three assertions seem justified: (1) the legality
of telling fortunes is in doubt in most North American jurisdictions; (2) Gypsies everywhere engage
in fortune-telling, usually with the knowledge of
the police; (3) the gap between these two situations
is bridged by complicated informal relationships
between the Gypsies and the police authorities.

Matters are, however, still further complicated
by rivalries among various Gypsy families and
"tribes." It is not at all unknown for the police,
probably in return for information and possibly
other considerations, to become party to intra-
Gypsy rivalries. This became particularly con-
spicuous in certain California localities in which
all Gypsy families except one were rigorously excluded from fortune-telling.

Over and above this normal involvement with
the police, which is expected of all Gypsies, there
are even more ambiguous relationships between
the authorities and certain Gypsy individuals. There
are a number of Gypsy special investigators, con-
sultants, "Gypsy kings," and other go-betweens
whose major activity is shuttling back and forth
between governmental authorites and Gypsies.
One such man, in California, serves as a consul-
tant to the relief authorities; his cooperation is
thought of by the Gypsies as essential for obtaining

relief payments. I have seen similar Gypsy go-
betweens in Eastern Europe, where such men
often hold minor positions within the Communist
Party or the government. In all the cases I have
seen, such men, while often praised by them in
public, are mistrusted and feared by the Gypsies.

Kinship Terminology
and the Bride-Price

In Table 1, I have indicated some differences between the ways in which the Gypsy and the English languages see the world of kinship relationships.

The Gypsy word <u>Rom</u> means husband, Gypsy, or man. But the category of "man" as used in English does not properly exist in the Gypsy language, since in ordinary conversation it is always necessary to specify whether one is talking about a Gypsy or a non-Gypsy. This is a linguistic reflection of the Gypsies' feeling of sacred separation from outsiders. The term <u>gaZo</u>, "outsider," differs from the current Yiddish term <u>goi</u> in that <u>gaZo</u> is not necessarily a pejorative, although such a meaning is often attached to it. Furthermore, <u>gaZo</u> is much more routinely and frequently used than is the word <u>goi</u>.

The other terms in Table 1 all deal with "affines" (the technical term for in-laws). In other domains, the Gypsy language divides the world into categories which are very similar to those provided by the English language—the Gypsies

Table 1
Some Gypsy words and their English equivalents

Gypsy	English	Comments
Rom	husband	
	Gypsy	
	man	Gypsy man
gaZo		non-Gypsy man
bori	sister-in-law	brother's wife
	daughter-in-law	
Zamutro	son-in-law	
	brother-in-law	sister's husband
kumnato		spouse's brother
paSo		wife's sister's husband
xanamik		child's spouse's parent

must have been greatly influenced by centuries of
living in the European language area. But the
Gypsy affinal terminology shows marked differences
from the English system. The semantic space
covered by our one word "brother-in-law" has three
Gypsy categories, that covered by the single Gypsy
word bori has two English categories, while the
the Gypsy word xanamik has no English equivalent
at all, though many other languages do have such
terms (Wayne Suttles, 1960, has suggested "co-
parent-in-law" as an English gloss). As it happens,
the Gypsy system of affinal terminology is very
closely related to a central institution of Gypsy
culture, the bride-price.

Marriages among Gypsies normally involve
the payment of a considerable sum of money by
the father of the groom to the father of the bride.
This bride-price may be as high as $8000, but the
average is closer to $2000. It is paid in recogni-
tion of the woman's role as the chief money earner,
but also as a material token and guarantee of the
seriousness of the marriage bond. Thus the fathers
of bride and groom become through the marriage
of their children "co-parents-in-law" (xanamikuria),
entering into a complex of financial and other reciprocal obligations that is expected to last a lifetime.

The themes of marriage, bride-price, and the
formation of a "co-parent-in-law" relationship have
a number of variations. The two future xanamikuria
may arrange the marriage more or less by themselves, without bothering too much about the views
of the young people involved. This is very rare;
it does happen this way some of the time in the
retelling of events by older men, but I suspect
that the prospecive groom and bride are always
consulted in one way or another.

The ideal method of arranging a marriage, from the point of view of the older people, is for the boy's father to pick a suitable family containing a suitable prospective bori (daughter-in-law), obtain the agreement of the prospective xanamik, then have the young people fall very much in love, and finally have everyone live happily with the resulting arrangement. But whether or not things actually work in the long run is always a problem. The relationship involves not only the groom and bride, but also, and perhaps primarily, their respective families. Should the marriage break up, especially within a year or so of having been contracted, disputes over the return of the bride-price are bound to arise. Very frequently only a portion of the bride-price is paid at the time of the wedding, with the balance due "when the xanamik can get the money." But if the marriage is not a happy one he is less likely to get it.

Another variation on the marriage-through-bride-price arrangement is elopement, naSimos. This happens in a substantial proportion of marriages. The two young people decide to get married, run away from home, and then leave their respective parents to work out the financial details later. There are some hints in the older literature to the effect that this was the favored form of marriage at one time.

We may now turn back to Table 1 with more of an understanding of the peculiarities of Gypsy affinal terminology. Let us take as an example the family relationship of Individual A (a male). From the point of view of the bride-price, which is the responsibility in a sense of A's entire family, his brother's wife and his son's wife occupy a very similar role: a woman for whom Individual A's

Gypsy wedding in Seattle, Washington, October 1969

family had to pay. Hence the Gypsies merge these relationships into a single term. On the other hand, English merges into one term types of "brother-in-law" for which the Gypsies require three. A sister's husband (Zamutro) is someone from whose family money has been received; this is not true of a spouse's brother (kumnato). Moreover, the husband of his wife's sister (paSo) shares with Individual A the same father-in-law, a man to whom the families of both sides to the paSo relationship had to pay money for their respective wives. The term Zamutro includes not only his sister's husband but also his son-in-law, both relationships indicating someone who has obtained a female from Individual A's family.

The relationship between language and culture, always expected by anthropologists, can thus be seen to be particularly close in the correspondence between Gypsy affinal terminology and the institution of the Gypsy bride-price. [2]

Inbreeding and the Bride-Price

Now and then in the course of discussing marriages
among Gypsies, Vania would mention a case in
which first cousins married. He would always ex-
press his disapproval of such practices. First-
cousin marriage, according to Vania and other
informants, is baro laZav (a big shame). But
once I examined every one of my recorded 199
marriages for a possible consanguinity between
the partners, I discovered that I had 9 cases of
first-cousin marriages and 19 other cases in which
the bride and groom were less closely, but still
definitely, related by blood. (Such unions, between
second cousins, for example, are not considered
shameful.) Since my information on the ancestors
of the recorded individuals is very incomplete,
and since the computer program can establish consanguinity only when it has information on the common ancestors of the partners, the proportion of
consanguineous unions is undoubtedly much higher
than my present figures would indicate.

If I take my known cases of first-cousin mar-

riages as a proportion only of those marriages on
which I have reasonably complete data for the ancestors of both spouses (I have listed 57 marriages
for which six or more of the spouses' grandparents
are known), I can estimate that first-cousin marriages represent about 16 percent of all Gypsy
marriages. A similar estimate of the proportion
of all consanguineous marriages--including such
relationships as second cousins and cousins once
removed--leads to the conclusion that about half
of all Gypsy marriages are contracted between
blood relatives.

The significance of this finding becomes clear
when we compare it with findings in other groups.
Cavalli-Sforza and Bodmer (1971, pp. 350-353)
show that this high degree of inbreeding (marriage
of blood relatives) is most unusual among human
groups. The very isolated small groups that are
similarly high in inbreeding fall far short of the
North American Gypsy population figures. For a
group of their size, the Gypsies may well be unique
in their degree of inbreeding.[3]

Figures 1 and 2 sketch some actual alliances
in order to illustrate the circumstances under
which consanguineous marriages take place. I
have followed the conventional practice of indicating
marriages by horizontal connecting lines under the
symbols of the respective individuals; sibling relationships are indicated by lines above symbols,
and parent-child relationships by vertical lines.
The numbers in or near the symbols identify individuals in my computer file. Circles indicate
females, and triangles indicate males. In Fig. 2,
I have also shown the coefficient of consanguinity
F (as a percentage) in the cases of the three consanguineous marriages. A figure of 6.25 indicates

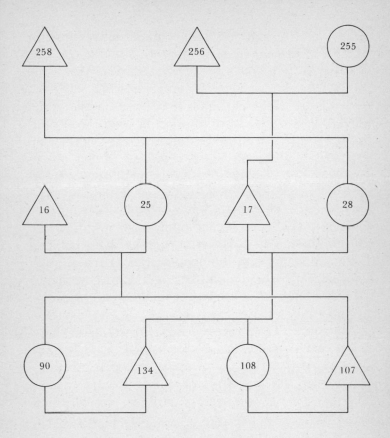

Fig. 1
First-cousin marriage and bride exchange

a full first cousin; lesser figures indicate lesser
relationships.

In Fig. 1 we see two marriages of cousins,
90-134 and 108-107. In neither case was a bride-
price paid. The girl 108 was considered an exchange for the girl 90; this arrangement is known
as paRuïmos (trade), and was facilitated by the
fact that the mothers of the two pairs were sisters.
I do not know of cases of trade except among close
relatives; I think it doubtful that unrelated families
would have enough confidence in one another to
enter into such an arrangement. Becoming co-
parents-in-law is difficult enough as it is; if things
do not work out with the couple, the financial and
emotional difficulties can last a lifetime, without
the added burden of having undertaken a trade.

The individuals numbered 16, 17, 256, and
255 in Fig. 1 are not necessary for an understanding
of the relationships I have discussed. I have shown
them merely to illustrate an important limitation
of my data: their incompleteness. I do not have
information concerning 16's parents, nor do I know
who 258's spouse was. I expect that as my data
base grows, some of these gaps will be filled in;
as this happens, my estimate of the percentage of
inbreeding among Gypsies will probably be raised.

In Fig. 2, I have shown a more complete pattern of marriage alliances. Number 98 is my
former principal informant, the man I call Stevano
in this essay. The diagram shows the many marriage alliances his children have with various offspring of numbers 12 and 14. Number 98's oldest
son is number 150, who married a daughter of
260-121. Once the co-parent-in-law relationship
was established, two further marriages took place
between children of 98-106 and 260-121. While

money changed hands for these alliances, there
was de facto some trading; it seems probable that
outstanding balances on the bride-price facilitated
this type of exchange. Several other unions took
place between 98's offspring and this family: 150's
second wife (176) is a relative of his first wife, as
are the spouses of 161 and 192. Number 196 married someone not descended from 12-14, but her
husband (207) is related (in ways too complicated
to show on this diagram) to 174 through the latter's
mother's side. It can also be seen that 207's family has had a previous alliance with the family
12-14 (marriage 68-117). The 12-14 family can
thus be seen as the meeting point through which
196 is tied to 207.

I draw the following tentative conclusions from
these data: the institution of the bride-price makes
it advantageous to marry more or less within the
family, since the burden of paying the price can
be alleviated through various reciprocal arrangements.[4] In the case of the exchange shown in Fig.
1, this mechanism operates very directly. But since
various family members usually get involved in
helping with bride-price payments, the more in-
direct payment circle suggested in Fig. 2 can also
be said to be a reciprocal arrangement. The very
youngest marriage of Fig. 2, that between 204 and
210, shows how sooner or later the ties between
two families resulted in consanguineous unions.

Previously I suggested that the Gypsy kinship
terminology is clarified by a consideration of the
bride-price institution. In this section, I have
suggested that the very high inbreeding coefficients
of the Gypsies are also related to this practice.
Furthermore, since it must be assumed that this
inbreeding has at least some consequences for the

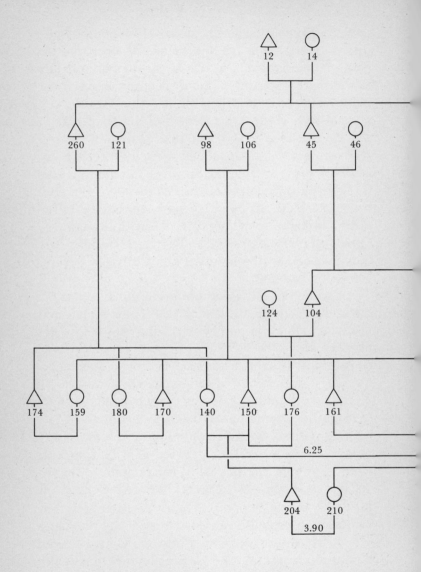

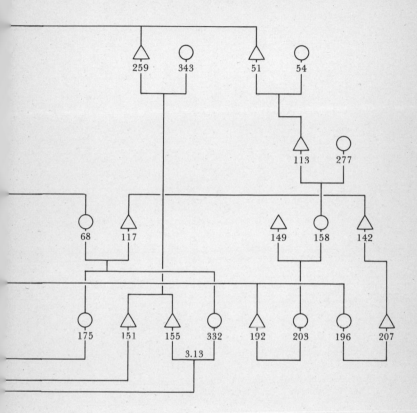

Fig. 2
Pattern of marriage alliances

gene pool of the Gypsies, these considerations
suggest a particular relationship between the cultural factor of bride-price and the biological factor
of the gene pool.

The Gypsies as an Institution of Western Culture

Why is it that despite the many pressures to assimilate to the world of non-Gypsies, the Gypsies retain so firmly their own culture? My answer is more a point of view than a substantiated fact, since, given the present state of our knowledge, the question does not allow itself to be resolved in a very simple or precise way.

It seems to me that the Gypsies persist because they, or groups like them, are needed in our culture. Their way of life provides solutions to some of our problems, and some individuals from among the non-Gypsies join them in each generation because they are attracted to the basic Gypsy values. Similarly, some Gypsies who find themselves out of sympathy with the Gypsy life leave to join the gaZe (non-Gypsies). The resulting selection of the Gypsy group provides a further strengthening of the distinctive Gypsy culture.

Neither joining nor leaving the Gypsy group could ever have been easy. Occasionally a Gypsy youngster becomes so disenchanted with his family's

Photo taken at a camp of *Rom* outside Bucarest, Romania, summer 1969

style of life that he falls in with non-Gypsy com-
panions and eventually leaves the group. The nature of my data, which deal with Gypsies who have
stayed Gypsies, precludes my knowing much about
those who leave the Gypsy way of life. I know of
a young boy now who has begun seeing non-Gypsy
girls and who may very well leave the Gypsy group
one day. But such cases are rare and difficult.
Gypsy children are not well trained to make their
way as gaZe.

Becoming a Gypsy is more difficult still. But
there are a number of Gypsy men (about six percent
of the grooms listed in my file) who married non-
Gypsy girls. (These marriages have a certain
attractiveness to the Gypsies because no bride-
price is paid under such circumstances.) Some
of these girls have become skillful fortune-tellers.
Most have learned to speak the Gypsy language
well, but some have not. I also know two non-
Gypsy men who have succeeded in entering the
Gypsy life through marriage; in these cases the
bride-price was paid by the young couples themselves after elopement.

My data indicate that under present conditions
in North America, the rate of inmarriage by non-
Gypsies is such that in the next generation of
Gypsies about three percent of its immediate parents will consist of newly inmarried non-Gypsies.
If we were to extrapolate this figure into the past,
assuming that the Gypsies have lived among Europeans for thirty generations, we would arrive at
an estimate of European ancestors among them
now of approximately 60 percent (0.97 raised to
the power of 30 yields a 40 percent proportion of
Indic ancestors). I cannot pretend to know anything
about the rate of intermarriage before the present

Photo taken at a camp of *Rom* outside Bucarest, Romania, summer 1969

period, but even if this estimate of a three percent
average rate of inmarriage over the generations
proved to be quite inaccurate, there would be little
doubt that a very sizable proportion of the Gypsies'
ancestors came from among Europeans.[5] While
many of North America's Gypsies have a vaguely
Indic appearance, most can probably pass as white
Americans.

Indeed the Gypsies are thoroughly European.
Not only does a majority of their ancestors probably come from old European stock, but the group
as a whole has also lived within the European culture area for many centuries. I suggest now that
in a certain manner of speaking each generation of
Gypsies has to make a decision whether or not to
remain Gypsy, and those non-Gypsies who become
part of the group have had to make a decision to
join. Of course these decisions are not made in
some ideal sense of "free will"; the choices are
made within the network of social conditions and
individual preferences. But whatever else this
network contains, it is evident that the differences
between the central values of Gypsies and non-
Gypsies play a role. In other words, I suggest that
the distinctively "Gypsy" ways of looking at the
world have helped to retain a core of Gypsies and
have helped to recruit an ever-renewing group of
non-Gypsies into the Gypsy world.

The differences between Gypsy and non-Gypsy
values can perhaps best be appreciated by briefly
considering attitudes toward business and toward
authority, and the Gypsy rejection of the non-Gypsy
world.

I have already described Gypsy methods of
business. In general, these do not concern themselves at all with performing services to clients;

customers are viewed as resources for obtaining
money, and no more. In much of the rest of Western culture, I suggest, there is considerable con-
flict and ambivalence between the mercenary and
the service aspects of business. On the one hand,
non-Gypsies are expected to be useful and helpful
to their clients, customers, and patients. But on
the other hand, the making of money and careers,
and the gaining of an advantage over the next man,
are powerful motives. I suggest that Gypsy culture
simplifies these choices, that it solves a problem
of ambivalence in this domain. The result is not
only a certain tension between Gypsies and those
non-Gypsies who come into contact with them, but
also a certain Gypsy spirit of forthrightness and
avoidance of hypocrisy.

I have reached similar conclusions about the
domain of authority. The Gypsies have no leaders,
no executive committees, no nationalist movement,
no Gypsy kings. Whenever the newspapers allege
such phenomena among the Gypsies, they have been
misled by certain individuals who engage in a more
or less elaborate play of deception. Gypsy attitudes
toward the politics and religion of non-Gypsies are
similarly cynical. They will often feign Christian
commitment and patriotism, but I know of no authenticated case of genuine Gypsy allegiance to
political or religious causes.[6] (This is not to
deny the possibility of cases involving isolated individuals; furthermore the situation may be different in the more acculturated groups of Europe.
For a discussion of these points, see Cohn, 1970.
For a description of the relationship between the
Rom and the anti-Nazi resistance during the Second
World War, see Yoors, 1971.)

If we look at the non-Gypsy world for attitudes

Photo taken at a camp of *Rom* in Timişoara, Romania, summer 1970

toward authority, the situation is surely much more
complex. On the one hand, there is much mobili-
zation behind governments, parties, and churches.
But on the other, there is also much evidence of a
dislike of all power and authority. Together with
a need to submit, there seems to be a need to resist (Cohn, 1958). By their rather unambiguous
rejection of the vanities of power and the slavish-
ness of submission, the Gypsies, in comparison
to the non-Gypsies surrounding them, again show
forthrightness and honesty.

Finally, the Gypsies have a strongly developed
sense of the integrity of their own culture and they
maintain a sacred separation from outsiders. The
Gypsies will not associate with outsiders socially;
the women avoid sexual contact with outsiders
rigorously and effectively; Gypsies do not enter a
non-Gypsy's home except on business. This sacred
separation is bolstered and made possible by all
the other attributes of Gypsy culture. The joy of
Gypsy feasts engenders pride and happiness that
one is not gaZo. The bride-price sets a tremen-
dous economic penalty for cases of desertion by
Gypsy women (I know of only one such case). The
Gypsy language, in which each Gypsy child I have
ever met in North America is absolutely fluent,
makes it possible to have a medium of communi-
cation that is impenetrable by outsiders. The
categories of this language do not admit of unspe-
cified "man" but insist on "Gypsy" versus "non-
Gypsy."

In short, the Gypsies reject our everyday
world and the values of our culture. This rejection, given a certain discontent of Western man,
has appeal to many people, and not only to Gypsies.
In conclusion, and if my suppositions are right,

these are the determinants of the Gypsies' persis-
tence in the non-Gypsy world: the Gypsy values
of business, Gypsy attitudes toward authority, the
Gypsy rejection of the Western world.   These are
all responses to Western dilemmas, given by Western men.

Postscript

I have come a long way since I met my first Gypsy
in Berlin. My Gypsy studies have opened new
fields to me: the Gypsy language has introduced
me to the world of Indo-European scholarship;
tangling with the complicated Gypsy genealogies
has led me to use the computer; the interesting
genetic questions raised by Gypsy inbreeding have
caused me to look into aspects of physical anthropology.

There have been non-intellectual benefits as
well. I have learned much from the Gypsy world
view. Perhaps alone among the peoples of Europe,
the Gypsies have been able to resist the tempta-
tions and vanities of power, the pretensions of
patriotism, religion, and ideology. Gypsies are
known to steal chickens and to cheat when selling
cars, but they have never organized a war, never
persecuted others, never manufactured bombs,
never perpetrated industrial pollution.

Notes

1. There is an analogous belief concerning "feral children," human infants supposed to have been abducted and reared by wolves. There are no authenticated cases on record, yet the stories persist. Bettelheim (1959) speculates that the myth is kept alive by the practice of some parents of abandoning children, for instance those with autistic symptoms, whose behavior is unacceptable to them. North America now has institutions in which such unfortunate children can be cared for, but these facilities were probably not so easily available in Europe one or two generations ago.

2. All the Gypsy terms for affinal relationships can be shown to have been borrowed from non-Gypsy languages. My original article on kinship terms (Cohn, 1969) indicates most of these sources; further relationships with non-Gypsy languages were shown by Markotic (1970). It is obvious that the items of the Gypsy kinship terminology are not completely different from other languages, either in the form the actual words take, or in the terri-

tories of meaning they respectively encompass.
But it is striking that the Gypsies have borrowed
selectively, taking a term here, a meaning there,
so that the whole fits into their system of social
organization.

One further point: the connection between language and social organization is always problema-
tical in at least two different ways. (1) Since we
do not have very good standards for judging what
would constitute a perfect fit between language and
culture, we cannot say just how good such a fit
is in a given case. Surely the Gypsies could get
along with a terminology less--or more--explicitly
related to their bride-price custom. All that we
can say definitely is that the Gypsy terminology
makes quite a bit more sense in Gypsy society
than it would in American society. (2) There is
also, in general, a problem of the direction of influence between language and social organization.
We cannot always be sure which has been more important in influencing the other. In the present case,
it may well be that the existence of this particular
terminology tends to strengthen the bride-price
custom, just as the custom itself favors the reten-
tion of the terminology.

3.   On the basis of my very incomplete data, which
must be considered as biased toward revealing less
inbreeding than there actually is, I estimate the
Gypsies' average coefficient of inbreeding $\bar{F}$ to be
at least 0.0118 but probably closer to 0.016. In
the general population, the coefficient is well below
0.001. Among U.S. Catholics, for whom there are
published data, the figure is 0.00009. For these
figures, and an explanation of their significance,
see Cavalli-Sforza and Bodmer (1971).

The amount of inbreeding found among Gypsies
may have deleterious consequences for general
health; it may also depress measured intelligence.
For discussion of these points, see Cavalli-Sforza
and Bodmer, 1971; Schull and Neel, 1965; Roberts,
1967; Morris, 1971; Symposium on "Methodology
of Isolates," 1964; and Goldschmidt, 1963. The
discussion by Morris is particularly cogent and
readable, and has the additional virtue of providing
the student with a critical discussion of some of the
other interpretations (pp. 413–415).

4.   As Figs. 1 and 2 illustrate, almost all Gypsy
marriages take place between members of the
same kindred, if we define kindred as comprising
all those individuals with whom a given individual
is related either through blood or through marriage.
The relatively high frequency of consanguineous
marriages, in my view, is only incidental to the
fact that marriage between members of the same
kindred is favored (practically to the exclusion of
any other). I have presented more evidence and
more discussion for this interpretation elsewhere
(Cohn, 1972b), where I also suggest that the kindred is much more important than the vitsa (tribe)
in Gypsy life.

5.   The evidence from physical anthropology does
not allow us, at this time, to estimate the proportion of genes which may have entered the Gypsy
gene pool from European sources. Boyd (1963)
thought that the "genetical method," by which he
meant ABO blood grouping, furnished "confirma-
tion of the Indian origin of the Gypsies." But his
opinion depended on a radical disregard of evidence
that had been carefully assembled by Mourant (1954).
Now there are new data from Sweden, as well as

a review of all the available evidence that is based on blood grouping (Beckman and Takman, 1965; Beckman, Takman, and Arfors, 1965). The result is that we now know that the Gypsies form a gene pool rather separate and distinct from that of non-Gypsies; moreover, this gene pool seems well differentiated with respect to separate Gypsy groups. But the extent of the Indic origin of this pool or pools is a moot point.

6.   While Gypsies in America never participate in any religious activities involving non-Gypsies, they do look upon catholic priests, in particular those of the Eastern Orthodox church, as having certain supernatural powers. They always have their infants baptized by a catholic priest, when possible by an Orthodox one. On the other hand, they show very little respect for the priests, regarding them more or less as necessary evils. This point is elaborated upon elsewhere (Cohn, 1970).

Suggestions for Further Reading

The book by Yoors (1967) is required reading for
anyone who wishes insight into the nature of Gypsy
culture. Yoors knows Gypsies as no other outsider
who has ever written on the subject does. In addition, Mitchell (1955) is instructive about Gypsy
business methods in New York. The unpublished
thesis by Cotten (1950) makes rewarding reading,
as does the work on Philadelphia Rom by Çoker
(1966).

The Gypsy language is authoritatively treated
by Gjerdman and Ljungberg (1963), but this important book is of more use to the expert than to
the student. The same can be said of the monu-
mental piece of scholarship by Sampson (1926),
which deals with a different dialect. The latter
work should be of special interest to students of
the other Indic languages.

Those who can read French should read the
book by Vaux de Foletier (1970), which is an in-
ventory of what the European documents tell us of
the arrival of Gypsies and of their life in Europe

up to the nineteenth century. For readers of German, there is the detailed account of the Nazi persecution of Gypsies in Döring (1964).

There are two specialized journals in the field of Gypsy studies: Etudes Tsiganes, published in Paris in French, and the Journal of the Gypsy Lore Society, published in Liverpool. The articles published in these journals are not of uniform quality. The student is advised to constantly ask himself, "How does the author know?" Unless a satisfactory answer suggests itself, it is best to maintain a certain skepticism. But if approached with a critical attitude, the back issues of these two journals can be a great source of knowledge.

References

Beckman, L., and J. Takman (1965). "On the anthropology of a Swedish Gypsy population." Hereditas, 53: 272-280.

Beckman, L., J. Takman, and K. E. Arfors (1965). "Distributions of blood and serum groups in a Swedish Gypsy population." Acta genetica et statistica medica, Basel, 15: 134-139.

Bettelheim, Bruno (1959). "Feral and autistic children." American Journal of Sociology, 64: 455-467.

Boyd, William C. (1963). "Four achievements of the genetical method in physical anthropology." American Anthropologist, 65: 243-252.

Calvet, Georges, Françoise Delvoye, and Michèle Labalette (1970). "Abrégé grammatical de manuš." Etudes Tsiganes, 16(1): 69-79.

Cavalli-Sforza, L. L., and W. F. Bodmer (1971). The Genetics of Human Populations. San Francisco: W. H. Freeman.

Cohn, Werner (1958). "Social stratification and the charismatic." Midwest Sociologist, 21: 12-18.

Cohn, Werner (1969). "Some comparisons between Gypsy (North American rom) and American English kinship terms." American Anthropologist, 71: 476-482.

Cohn, Werner (1970). "La persistance d'un groupe paria relativement stable: quelques réflexions sur les Tsiganes nord-américains." Etudes Tsiganes, 16(2-3): 3-23.

Cohn, Werner (1972a). "Marko and Moso. A Gypsy tale from Canada told by Biga." Journal of the Gypsy Lore Society, 51(1-2): 13-27.

Cohn, Werner (1972b). "Marriage chez les Rom nord-américains: quelques conséquences du 'prix de la mariée'." Etudes Tsiganes, 18(2-3): 4-11.

Cohn, Werner (n.d.). "Gypsy categories of men: lexicon and attitudes." Mimeographed.

Cotten, Rena Maxine (1950). "The fork in the road: a study of acculturation among the kalderaš Gypsies." Ph.D. thesis, Columbia University.

Çoker, Gülbün (1966). "Romany Rye in Philadelphia: a sequel." Southwestern Journal of Anthropology, 22: 85-100.

Döring, Hans-Joachim (1964). "Die Zigeuner im Nationalsozialistischen Staat." Hamburg: Kriminalistik Verlag.

Gjerdman, Olof, and Erik Ljungberg (1963). "The language of the Swedish coppersmith Gypsy Johan Dimitri Taikon." Uppsala, A-B Lundequistska.

Goldschmidt, Elisabeth, ed. (1963). The Genetics
of Migrant and Isolate Populations. Baltimore:
Williams and Wilkins, on behalf of the Association
for the Aid of Crippled Children.

Gudschinsky, Sarah C. (1967). How to Learn an
Unwritten Language. New York: Holt, Rinehart,
and Winston.

Jean, Daniel (1970). "Glossaire de gadškeno manus."
Etudes Tsiganes, 16(1): 4-68.

Markotic, Vladimir (1970). "North American
Gypsy terms: a comment." American Anthropologist, 72: 847-848.

Ministry of Housing and Local Government, Welsh
Office (1967). "Gypsies and other travellers."
London: H. M. Stationery Office.

Mitchell, Joseph (1955). "Profiles--the beautiful
flower." New Yorker, 31: 39-81.

Morris, Laura Newell (1971). Human Populations,
Genetic Variation, and Evolution. San Francisco:
Chandler.

Mourant, A. E. (1954). The Distribution of the
Human Blood Groups. Oxford: Blackwell Scien-
tific Publications.

Roberts, D. F. (1967). "Incest, inbreeding, and
mental abilities." British Medical Journal, 4:
336-337.

Sampson, John (1926). The Dialect of the Gypsies
of Wales. Oxford: Oxford University Press.

Schull, William J., and James V. Neel (1965).
The Effects of Inbreeding on Japanese Children.
New York: Harper and Row.

Suttles, Wayne (1960). "Affinal ties, subsistence, and prestige among the Coast Salish." American Anthropologist, 62: 296-305.

Symposium on "Methodology of Isolates" (1964). Organized by the Problem Commission of Neurogenetics of the World Federation on Neurology. Basel: S. Karger.

Vaux de Foletier, Francois de (1970). Mille Ans d'Histoire des Tsiganes. Paris: Fayard.

Yoors, Jan (1967). The Gypsies. New York: Simon and Schuster.

Yoors, Jan (1971). Crossing. New York: Simon and Schuster.

Index